VIENNA'S CONSCIENCE

CLOSE-UPS AND CONVERSATIONS AFTER HITLER

RICHARD WINTER

SUSAN WINTER BALK

GREGORY WEEKS

REEDY PRESS
St. Louis, Missouri

Reedy Press
PO Box 5131
St. Louis, MO 63139
USA

Library of Congress Control Number: 2007934941
ISBN: 978-1-933370-08-8

For information on all Reedy Press publications visit our website at www.reedypress.com.

Printed in Canada
07 08 09 10 11 5 4 3 2 1

Photographs from 1938 courtesy the Vienna Police Department.

Because Richard Winter died in September 2000, before *Vienna's Conscience* was finished, he was unable to make final edits and corrections. Some attributions may be incorrect due to lost notes. However, best efforts to avoid errors and omissions and to contact everyone who appears in this book were made.

CONTENTS

ACKNOWLEDGMENTS

Special thanks to Ken Balk.

Thanks also to the following people, without whose contributions and support this book could not exist:

- Tom Passavant for getting the project started

- Jim Margolis and Tom Smolka for their photographic memories, laser wits, and brotherly love

- Dean David Wilson, Professor Gregory Weeks, and Professor Warren Rosenblum of Webster University in St. Louis and Vienna for their vision and hard work

- Christine Salmen, of Webster University in St. Louis and Vienna, for her translation and enthusiasm

- Jay Balk, Page Ashley, and Marvin Klamen for their steady resourcefulness, advice, and freindship

- Aden Stern and Rachel Anderson for their childhood curiosity about the Holocaust

- Dr. Hannah Kapit for her enduring friendship and for many stories about Vienna and the Viennese

- Matt Heidenry and Josh Stevens for bringing this book to life

- Warren Rosenblum, Frank Roth, Alan Bortz, and Jean Cavender and Daniel Reich of the St. Louis Holocaust Museum, for bringing the traveling exhibit of *Vienna's Conscience* to life

PREFACE

One winter day in 2005, five years after my late husband, Richard Winter's death, I got a call from Webster University's Dean of Arts and Sciences David Wilson. The dean, who was aware that my late husband had escaped from Vienna on his third try in 1938, told me that Gregory Weeks, a professor at Webster's Vienna campus, would be in St. Louis to lecture on the topic of Nazi connections to the Austrian police.

I went to the lecture and was greatly impressed by Weeks's powerful presentation. My friend Ken Balk—now my husband—invited Weeks, Professor Warren Rosenblum, and Dean Wilson to his home for lunch a few days later. In the course of the conversation about Vienna and the Viennese, I thought of Richard's photographs and interviews from 1988. After some searching, I found them and passed them around.

Professor Weeks suggested trying to publish them, noting that they would be received now with a level of interest that would not have existed in 1988. He pointed out that Austria is now coming to grips with its past, teaching the Holocaust in the schools, issuing apologies, and making reparations. Rosenblum was similarly encouraging.

Weeks returned to Austria and regularly sent me notes encouraging me to publish the project. Dean Wilson eventually introduced me to the principals of Reedy Press. They too were enthusiastic about the promise of a project based on the photographs and interviews. I was delighted. My first thought was that Weeks should place the nearly twenty-year-old document in historical context. He graciously agreed.

Momentum gained, as Webster students and faculty alike became involved in various aspects of the project. Christine Salmen, a visiting student and instructor in St. Louis from Vienna, translated the interviews from German to English. Professor Rosenblum arranged a traveling exhibit of the photographs and English translations of the interviews that would begin at the Holocaust Museum in St. Louis simultaneously with the release of this book.

My late husband would be delighted at the interest and support of a project that grew out of his personal attempt to come to terms with the citizens of the city of his birth for which he felt such passionate ambivalence.

Ricki's personal goal was to encourage study and understanding of the source of hate crimes and crimes against humanity and to promote the peaceful resolution of conflicts based on such crimes. His hope was to prevent them from escalating into violence born of ignorance. He would be horrified to know that we, the world community, have not done very well at enforcing "Never Again."

Historian Gregory Weeks, as he made the last revisions and wrote the last lines of his contribution to this book, sent me an email that reads in part:

> I was sitting in a hotel in Sarajevo, a city that was bombarded for months by Serbian soldiers and where it took almost ten years for NATO to intervene to stop the killing. Walking down the street one afternoon, I saw a man missing both of his legs rolling himself through the pedestrian zone in a wheelchair and a woman with an amputated leg stopping with her son to chat with a friend at a cafe. These people are traumatized. The war has left deep marks.

The same was true in Austria in 1988, and even now, 70 years later, the Austrians are still figuring out how to approach all of this.

What is the moral and right thing to do? How should one address these topics? What significance do the conversations that Ricki had with these strangers on the street have for Austrians and the rest of us today? These are deep questions, and I suppose every reader will have to form his or her own opinion, but here is what it means for me:

> My feeling is that these conversations offer a window for understanding how people cope with trauma, both as victims and perpetrators, and that admitting guilt or at least some measure of responsibility is important for reconciliation, and without reconciliation, the scars can never heal. There can be no closure without realization that wrong has been done and that crimes have been committed. Some Austrians still fail to recognize this over sixty years after the end of World War II; however, they are becoming fewer and fewer by the day. Will people show moral strength and conscience or will they bow to the pressure of the masses? Will they save a life or sacrifice it for their own? These are tough questions and ones that we cannot answer until we are put in those situations.

—Susan Winter Balk

CHANGE OVER TIME

REMEMBERING AND FORGETTING IN VIENNA, 1938–1988–2008

BY GREGORY WEEKS

Flashback: March 1938, "Vienna, Germany"—It has a strange ring to it, but after the Nazi annexation of Austria, Vienna is now the second-largest city in "Greater Germany." Adolf Hitler has arrived in Vienna. The forced unification of Austria with Germany, the Anschluss, is reality. Vienna, with its population of 1.8 million souls, is now part of Adolf Hitler's growing empire, and Hitler has promised to turn the city into the pearl that he thinks it ought to be. Author Thomas Weyr describes it as a pearl that was receiving a new setting,[1] one draped in Swastika flags.

The expressions of either dismay or jubilation are etched on the faces of the Viennese in the black and white photographs from 1938, but is it possible to understand what happened in Austria in that year? Are common perceptions of the Anschluss correct? And is it possible to truly grasp what it was like to be there—the emotions, the confusion, the anger, the frustration? There were certainly those Viennese who opposed the Anschluss, but there were many more who welcomed it and reveled in the streets, delighting in anti-Semitism and tormenting their Jewish neighbors.[2]

The Anschluss was precipitated by the policies of National Socialist Germany under Adolf Hitler after his rise to power in Germany in 1933. It was Hitler's stated goal to unite the German-speaking peoples of Germany and Austria in a *Volksgemeinschaft*, a peoples' community, under his leadership. Hitler made a concerted and successful effort to undermine the Austrian economy until the final annexation of Austria in March 1938. Not only did German National Socialists undermine the economy of the country, but they also supported a terror campaign waged by Austrian Nazis against political parties opposed to their views and against the government of Austria, especially after 1934.[3]

The idea of an Anschluss uniting Germany and Austria had always been talked about but had never been realized. In 1866, when the Habsburgs vied for control over the southern German states with Prussia, the two countries went to war over the question of what would be greater Germany (*Grossdeutsch*) and what would be smaller Germany (*Kleindeutsch*). In this period, the Austrians pushed for a greater German solution. These dreams were dashed after the Austrian defeat at the

Battle of Königgrätz in 1866. Because the Habsburg Empire had been
so weakened by this defeat, Emperor Franz Josef I chose to give greater
autonomy to the Hungarian part of the empire, thus establishing the dual
monarchy. Of course, this left the Czechs, the third-largest population
group in the empire, out of the deal, and there were continual problems
with Czech demands for a greater voice in the affairs of the monarchy.

The late nineteenth and early twentieth centuries were an age of
nationalism for Austrians, Jew and non-Jew alike. It was an age that
culminated in a battle over nationalistic ideals in the First World
War and that destroyed the multiethnic dual monarchy in 1918. The
Anschluss could easily have occurred in 1918, but it did not due to Allied

intervention. It took Hitler and his rise in Germany to finally "solve" "the German Question." Most nationalist Austrians were in favor of joining Germany, not in an annexation but in a union. Greater Germany had always been a dream held by the Austrian pan-German movement and was in direct opposition to pan-Slavism and other nationalist movements of the pre– and post–World War I period in Central Europe. There were certainly problems in the period prior to 1918, but the real problems for Austria began with the end of the First World War and the collapse of Austria-Hungary.

The First World War put an end to the old regimes of Europe, including the Austro-Hungarian dual monarchy. The last Austrian emperor abdicated in November 1918, and upon his departure, there were renewed calls for unification with Germany. The World War I aftermath, where the lands of the dual monarchy were split under U.S. President Woodrow Wilson's self-determination plans, left only a tiny "rump" Austria that had to redefine its identity.

Austria's transition from an economic and political superpower to a nation of 6 million is key to comprehending how Austrians felt during the years 1918 to 1938. The economic chaos and problematic reparations payments to the Allied Powers following World War I must be taken into account. The reworked Austria was left without sufficient industrial or agricultural capacity. Added to this were the political upheaval with the abdication of the last Habsburg emperor, Kaiser Karl, in 1918; the establishment of the Austrian First Republic in that same year; the currency switch from crowns to schillings; and the high inflation. Austria's first move was to declare itself *Deutsch-Österreich* (German-Austria) and attempt unification with Germany, but the Allies would not permit this, and thus, little Austria was left to its own devices and entirely to its own means.

Adolf Hitler, who had fought in the First World War, subscribed to this idea, and with his rise to power as chancellor of Germany in 1933, a born Austrian would finally make the move to unite the two German-speaking nations. It was a matter of pride for many Austrians to return their homeland to its former greatness and grandeur, but in the beginning, no one knew of the dark side of Hitler's plans, of the anti-Semitism and discrimination that would later be implemented under his leadership.

After Austria suffered first a Socialist revolt in February 1934 and
a National Socialist one in July that same year, it became clear that
Hitler was working to undermine the Austro-fascist corporatist state
under Chancellor Engelbert Dollfuss. Dollfuss was killed by an Austrian
SS brigade in the July revolt, and his successor, Kurt Schuschnigg, did
everything in his power to stem the impending takeover, to no avail.
Benito Mussolini, the fascist leader of Italy, at first supported the
Austrians, but eventually, on a cooperation course with Hitler, he chose to
stand by and do nothing. Pressure on Austria from Germany increased.
Leaflets were distributed in border areas calling on Austrians to support
Germany, and Austria, dependent on tourism, was dealt a virtual death
blow with a thousand-mark tax on anyone wishing to enter the country
from Germany. This virtually ended tourism and even family visits, and
weakened the Austrian economy so severely that it became increasingly
easy for Hitler to carry through with his plans for annexation.[4]

Without an understanding of how Austria developed from 1866 to 1938, it is impossible to understand the immense appeal of Hitler and the Nazis. The political upheaval prior to and following the First World War unsettled Austrian society and made the political scene volatile and unstable. This was the era in which political anti-Semitism prevailed in Austria and the era in which Hitler was raised and attended school. It was also the era of art and culture known as *fin de siècle* or *Jugendstil* or *Art Nouveau*, and then *Art Deco*. Turbulent times either deaden or produce great art. Turbulence was evident in Vienna prior to the German invasion and Hitler's seizure of power in Austria. When Hitler arrived in Austria, there were 600,000 unemployed, and Vienna, despite all of its social programs, was still recovering from the world economic crisis of the 1930s. Unlike Germany, Austria really was seized. Hitler was not elected. That does not mean that a majority of Austrians were not pleased or happy to welcome him. The throngs of Austrians on the Heldenplatz belie the postwar myth that Austria was the first victim of National Socialist aggression.[5]

Vienna was Adolf Hitler's muse. Hitler's Vienna years had a huge impact on his later thinking and his anti-Semitism. His path to the halls of power as chancellor of the German Reich could never have occurred without the lessons he learned in Vienna. On the one hand, Vienna moved Hitler with its art, culture, and opera, but on the other hand, Vienna gave Hitler the examples of the virulent anti-Semitism that he imitated in his later career.

It is crucial to remember that the expulsion of the Austrian Jews after 1938 is mostly a story of the City of Vienna, since on March 13, 1938, 167,242 of Austria's 206,000 Jews lived within the city's limits and only 14,633 in the other Austrian federal states. In addition to this number, there were 24,118 non-practicing Jews in Austria.[6] According to numerous eyewitnesses, the humiliation was the worst to bear in Vienna after the Anschluss.[7] The degradation of those the regime viewed as its enemies was a special burden. Those persecuted in this manner often committed suicide, and suicide rates in Vienna soared.[8] Historian Gerhard Botz calculates that suicides in March 1938 were three times higher than the years before and that the increased number of suicides in

Vienna reached its highest point in April 1988. Of course, some of these "suicides" were actually murders by the SS, as was clearly the case with the Austrian Jewish General Wilhelm Zehner in 1938.[9] Of suicides in the month between March 12, 1938, and April 11, 1938, 42 percent were Jewish.[10] One of the political opponents of the Nazis who emigrated, Austrian author and PEN club member Franz Theodor Csokor said repeatedly that he would rather die than live one moment under Nazi tyranny.[11] Many of those committing suicide probably felt the same way.

Those who could, fled. Those who could not, sought other ways of coping with the stress. All were forced to forever leave everything they had known and loved. Lives were destroyed, lives were interrupted, and lives were changed by circumstances beyond their control and beyond their power to cope.

Even when refugees did manage to escape Nazi-controlled Vienna, they had to pay an exit tax that amounted almost exactly to the total value of all their property. The machinery of Nazi legislation made this possible. The refugees were stripped of everything they possessed, and if they stayed or were unable to leave, they were deported and eventually murdered by gassing, or they perished from starvation or disease.

In the end, German-Austria did not survive, nor did Hitler's Third Reich. Vienna was separated from Germany in 1945, and Germany and Austria were divided among the Allies. The Austrian struggle for a post–World War I identity was decided for them, first by Germany's invasion in 1938, which brutally ended Austria's First Republic and the fascist Austrian Corporate State, which had lasted only from 1934 until the German takeover in 1938, and then by the forced removal of German influence by the Allies following the end of World War II.

The Nazis destroyed much of the old Vienna. In seven short years, Austria had been transformed from imperial glory to ashes and rubble. Was this the setting of the pearl Hitler had intended? In the process, Austria had lost some of its greatest minds, its greatest assets, and its future. Those minds would never be regained. Many of the surviving refugees chose not to return. Some would revisit Vienna, but they could never really be part of its social fabric again. They were outsiders, foreigners and strangers in their own land.

Fast Forward: 1988, Vienna—Refugee Richard Winter brings his camera and tape recorder back to Vienna and approaches strangers on the street. He asks them what they like most about Austria. It is clear that he still loves the city he was forced to leave in 1938—the cafes, the streets, the cuisine, even the people. Then, abruptly, suddenly, Winter shifts his line of questioning. He asks these strangers what they think of the Jews having been forced to leave Vienna after the Anschluss. The answers he receives range from the ordinary to the revolting. One woman tells him that Americans should worry about their own "Indians" and "Negroes" and that the Austrians will worry about "their Jews."

Fifty years after the end of World War II, there were still former Nazis on the streets of Vienna. They did not wear Nazi uniforms or give Hitler salutes, but they were there and their opinions had changed very little, despite a lost war and the suffering that had accompanied it.

In 1986, Dr. Kurt Waldheim had been elected Austrian federal president despite revelations about his wartime past, serving as a soldier in Hitler's army in the Balkans. Two years later, Austria was still mired in this discussion as the result of Waldheim being placed on a U.S. watchlist. Waldheim unwillingly and unwittingly opened the floodgates to Austria's problematic past, and in the beginning, he did not or could not recognize that he had been a vital part of the machinery that led to the murder of nearly 66,000 Austrian Jews. His repeated statement to Green Party politician Freda Meissner-Blau in 1986, "But I didn't do anything" shows his lack of recognition about his role.[12] In fact, Waldheim's inability to take a clear stand on his wartime years may have been his greatest contribution to Austrian politics because it began one of the most important debates of the post–World War II Austrian Second Republic, one that continues to this day.

The journalist Hubertus Czernin was not the first to discover the gaps in Waldheim's official biography, but he was the first to investigate the charges that Waldheim had belonged to the SA, the brown shirts, and had been present in Bosnia and Saloniki, where war crimes were committed. He asked permission of Waldheim to look at his military record in the Austrian State Archives, which Waldheim promply gave.

In the file, Czernin found that Waldheim was listed as both a member of the SA and the National Socialist Student League (NS-Studentenbund).

At the same time, an amateur historian who was a Social Democrat from Innsbruck discovered and purchased a photo in an antique shop that showed Waldheim in his army uniform beside SS Gruppenführer Arthur Phelps in Podgorica, Bosnia. The dam broke and additional details about Waldheim's past were revealed: He had been on the staff of the executed war criminal General Alexander Löhr, had received the Zvonimir medal from the Croatian Ustascha Regime, which was allied with the Nazis, and had served from 1942 onward as a translator in the Kampfgruppe Western Bosnia within Army Group E.[13]

Waldheim, who had risen in the Austrian Foreign Ministry and had eventually become secretary general of the United Nations, left out significant portions of his biography, and these would come back to haunt him during the 1986 Austrian presidential campaign. Even after his death in 2007, Waldheim's wartime activities are still a matter of extreme controversy in Austria. There are some who vilify him and others who see him as typical of the wartime generation. Certainly, Waldheim did not have the courage to speak out against the Nazi regime, but he was also never directly implicated in war crimes.[14] The main charges against him were that he conveniently left out portions of his biography that placed him in areas where war crimes had been committed.

There were many Waldheims—people who either were passive bystanders and witnesses to the crimes of the National Socialists or, like Waldheim, were drafted into the armed forces and served on fronts throughout Europe and in North Africa. As Waldheim himself phrased it, "I only did my duty."

In the firm belief that he was not a criminal, Waldheim failed to realize that his denial of involvement could be interpreted as complicity by those who had been victimized, and he became the target of attacks from all sides as a public personality.

Richard Winter in Vienna, 1938

To further exacerbate the situation of the Waldheim Affair and the Remembrance Year 1988, playwright Thomas Bernhard's *Heldenplatz* about the Anschluss was on stage at Vienna's renowned Burgtheater.[15] Opinions diverged greatly about the play, even from those who had yet to see it performed. The play polarized the public in 1988. The space Heldenplatz itself, the Place of Heroes, has a special significance in Austrian history that both unites and divides generations. The Heldenplatz is the place where the emperors lived, the Habsburg winter palace. At the same time, it is also the place where Hitler spoke to the masses after Austria's annexation in 1938 and the place where Austrians protested the anti-foreigner sentiments of the populist Freedom Party with a chain of candles in the 1990s.

The Heldenplatz is a place of special significance, historically, politically, and socially. It represents the best and worst of Austrian politics and culture. It is an inescapable part of the Austrian psyche, and it has immense relevance to any discussion of changes in Austrian culture since 1938 and for understanding Bernhard's play of the same name and the controversy surrounding it in 1988.

In 1988, most Austrians spent little time reflecting on the past—on the crimes of the Nazi regime on Austrian territory, or on other wartime fronts where former Austrians, now with German citizenship and wearing German uniforms, were stationed. There seemed to be an unwritten rule that a common front should be presented to the outside world.

The significance of the Heldenplatz in Austrian history is immense. Thomas Bernhard well knew this when he chose the title for his play and made emigration from German-controlled Austria a theme. The diction of his characters was a clear provocation of his Austrian audience. *Heldenplatz* was the last play to be written by Bernhard before he died in 1989. It was first performed at Vienna's Burgtheater on November 4, 1988, under the direction of Claus Peymann, after a lengthy delay and a venomous press campaign against it. Reviews from the period, including those in the English-language press, were generally critical of the play. At the first performance, despite catcalls and boos from some members of the audience, there was a forty-minute standing ovation at the end, where both Peymann and Bernhard were present on the stage.[16]

The play tells the story of an Austrian emigrant, Professor Josef Schuster, through his family after he has returned to Vienna and committed suicide because he cannot cope with how little Austria has changed and how he is treated by other Austrians. Statements attributed to Professor Schuster by his family members are sharply critical of Austria and its past and proved to be offensive to many Austrians who saw the comments of the play's protagonist as a slur to their national honor. Although most Americans have never heard of Bernhard's play or the controversy surrounding it, an understanding of it is crucial to understanding the debates of the year 1988 and their importance for Austrian history.

At the same time that Bernhard was harshly criticizing Austria through his characters in *Heldenplatz*, the Republic of Austria was commemorating the events of 1938 in an educational brochure by Gustav Spann and Peter Malina for public distribution titled 1938 1988. The pamphlet featured a black and white photograph of a young Austrian from 1938 juxtaposed with a color photograph of a young Austrian of the same age and stature from half a century later. The message was clear: Those alive in 1938 were like us. They were caught up in the turbulence of events and had to make difficult choices.[17]

There was some attempt to use 1988, the fiftieth anniversary of the Anschluss, as a teaching tool, at least by the politicians in the Ministry of Education and Culture. This was the political face of Austria, the way Austria wanted itself to be portrayed to the outside world. Unfortunately, it was not the public face of the nation at the personal level, the way Austrians on the street viewed what happened in 1938. The Austria of the common people, this other Austria, this other Vienna, was the one that Richard Winter documented in his photographs and interviews, the ones that Austrian politicians did not want to see but which the outside world was seeing and hearing about frequently on the nightly news.

Nineteen-eighty-eight was a time of political and historical introspection and retrospection in some circles and a time of denial in others. Austria was coming to terms with its wartime past, albeit slowly. As some denied, others commemorated. The City of Vienna hosted the second year of its new *Wiener Vorlesungen* (Vienna Lecture Series) with the overarching theme "Dealing with History." Perhaps this series should have been called "Confronting History," but that would not have truly reflected the Viennese mood, which was simply to cursorily dismiss the "problem" and move on. In 1988, memories of 1938 were still so strong that this Austrian past could not be "dealt with," at least not in a lecture series. The wounds were fresh, and they touched a raw nerve. Even after fifty years, no one talked openly about what happened. Older Viennese were in denial. Younger Viennese were embarrassed. The Nazi era still extended a shadow that darkened even the brightest Viennese day.

The lives destroyed and interrupted, the dreams broken, and the hopes dashed tell one aspect of Vienna in 1938. Another part of the story concerns opportunists, greed, the coveting of neighbors' property, and the quick rise of National Socialists to high positions. A third aspect of the story of 1938 Vienna tells of those, like Richard Winter, who were forced to leave. They loved Vienna as their home and could never forgive the Nazis and their fellow Austrians for having taken this away from them. And perhaps naïvely, they nursed the hope that those who had supported the Anschluss, as well as the next generation, would acknowledge their mistakes and those of their parents.

Author Ruth Kluger wrote, "Vienna was a city with no exit, a city that banished you and then didn't allow you to leave."[18] This was certainly true in Richard Winter's case. He attempted to flee Vienna three times and finally succeeded on his last try. This was true of thousands of other refugees as well. Those attempting to exit had to run the gamut of various authorities waiting for their requests, from proving their citizenship and that they did not owe anything to "aryans," paying taxes designed to take their savings, and lining up to get emigration visas for countries known and unknown.

To leave Vienna, émigrés were put through the mills of a bureaucracy designed with murderous efficiency under the Nazis. Hurdles were added every step of the way. One survivor described it as living in a real life Kafka novel: You were charged with an unknown crime; you ran from authority to authority trying to prove your innocence, but that was impossible since you had no idea of your transgression. The process was at times so complicated that it seemed impossible to ever leave at all.

The first earnest attempts by Austrians to face the past came in 1988 in the wake of the "Waldheim Affair," but the truly pivotal moments in Austrian political efforts at reconciliation came in 1992 and 1993 when then-Chancellor Franz Vranitzky and Austrian President Thomas Klestil both publicly apologized for the wrongs committed by Austrians under the Nazi dictatorship from 1938 to 1945. This still was not full disclosure, but it was a beginning, and Austria has increasingly tried to face the charges that have been leveled against its people, that they were not merely victims and that they were often complicit in the crimes of National Socialism.

Sadly, all of this was long after Richard Winter had visited Vienna. In 1988, it must have seemed to him that little had changed. A large number of Nazis who had aryanized businesses in 1938 still owned them, and no one seemed sorry that Winter had been forced to flee. It was like the old Cabaret scene where Helmut Qualtinger's character Herr Karl is approached by his former Jewish neighbor, Tennenbaum, and Herr Karl asks, "Where were you for so long?" as if nothing at all had happened. This is a reflection of the post–World War II Austrian psyche: Act as if nothing has happened, and perhaps everything will be all right; but too much damage had been done, and there are too many unanswered questions.[19]

The shards are there, embedded in the memories and in the denials of those who walked the streets during the Third Reich and of those who left or were left behind. These are powerful, even explosive memories, and they must be recognized and reconciled.

In general, Austrian Nazis never really felt ashamed of what they had done. The first part of the Moscow Declaration of 1943, which stated that Austria was the "first victim of fascist aggression," gave these unrepentant criminals an excuse to sweep everything under the rug. Austria's Nazis and some politicians conveniently forgot the second part of the declaration that stated that Austria had a duty to atone for the crimes that had occurred under Nazi rule. The Moscow Declaration became the perfect excuse for Austrians not to atone for the crimes that were committed by their people and on their territory after the Anschluss. It was a made-to-order excuse, courtesy of the Allied Powers.[20]

Some claim that the inability of Nazis to mourn Hitler created a situation in which he was secretly idolized and in which Austrians could not find a proper coping behavior to account for their deeds under his leadership,[21] but it seems that it is less the inability to mourn Hitler than the inability to distance themselves from their families and the general numbness that resulted from the war that embedded and internalized itself in the minds and everyday experiences of the Austrians in the postwar era.[22] Günter Grass has a chapter in *The Tin Drum* titled "In the Onion Cellar" where Germans go to chop up onions so that they can cry since they are no longer able to shed tears on their own.[23] This certainly reminds us of the Viennese experience. Numbness, lack of feeling, and being pushed along by the wave that characterized Vienna in 1938. As Peter Sichrovsky states, "The silence of the perpetrators can become a time bomb. An entire generation, a generation torn between the reality of an external new democracy and old fascistic family ideals, failed to assimilate the past, and because of this failure, it could not forge a new identity, one that would make a recurrence of the past unimaginable. Nearly all of the people I [Sichrovsky] interviewed, regardless of their attitude toward their [Nazi] parents were convinced that what happened under the Nazis could recur."[24]

Austria's priorities were reflected in the behavior of its citizens from the end of World War II onward. The Austrian response was to gloss over or ignore Austrian involvement in the crimes of Nazi Germany and skillfully manipulate the Moscow Declaration of 1943 to relieve themselves of the Nazi burden.

Vienna was invaded by Germans, not all of whom were Nazis, but who willingly served a regime that had genocide as its main political and social focus. The same was true of the Austrians. There were those who joined the Nazis and those who did not, but either way, whether bystander or party member, all were either witnesses to or participants in one of the greatest crimes of the twentieth century.

The old, unrepentant Nazis remained unrepentant until their dying days. The younger generations, the children of Nazis and anti-Nazis, confronted these admirers of Hitler and forced change. The photos taken by Richard Winter in 1988 are representative of these three generations. There are students and retirees, businesspeople and shop owners, bartenders and policemen. These are the faces of Austria in 1988, of those who are regretful but not apologetic and those who are neither. These faces show what Historian Robert Knight has dubbed the "Contours of Memory in Post-Nazi Austria."[25]

Since then, there has been a great deal of soul searching on all sides, prompted by lawsuits, restitution claims, and attempts to finally "draw a line" under this uncomfortable discussion of Austrians' World War II involvement.[26] Austrians are not Germans, and they have made this very clear since 1945. Before 1945, however, many Austrians wanted to be German. This paradox centers on the question of Austrian national identity and how Austrians want themselves to be viewed.

The Austrian trauma of 1938 never ended. It simply continued into the post–World War II period and continues to this very day. The majority of Viennese have relegated their past to old photo albums and memories, but for èmigrès like Richard Winter, this past was and is still very much alive. In a sense, banning memories to old photo albums allows Austrians to continue forward since it lets them start anew by relegating uncomfortable thoughts to another realm, a conveniently packaged one that limits the damage that can be done to them when past deeds become a topic of conversation.

The perennial debate continues: Was Austria a vanquished victim or were Austrians perpetrators and persecutors? There is some truth in both views, but more it seems in the second. Austrian creativity in dealing with these issues gave way to a whitewash that was exposed with the election of Kurt Waldheim as Austrian federal president in 1986. Most Austrians knew about the Holocaust and what had happened in Vienna, but they denied it. When they were forced to admit their past transgressions, the Austrians sugar-coated the pill, but sugar-coating this era did not make the bitter medicine go down any more easily. The truth was difficult to swallow, and the Austrians are still in the process of forcing it down.

Austria had many good people in 1938 who chose to do nothing. They did not act. Others turned bad. Why? Psychologist Philip Zimbardo offers an answer.[27] When an interviewer from the *New York Times* asked him, "So you disagree with Anne Frank, who wrote in her diary, 'I still believe, in spite of everything, that people are truly good at heart'?" Zimbardo answered, "That's not true. Some people can be made into monsters. And the people who abused, and killed her, were."[28]

Did the Austrians with whom Winter conversed on the streets of Vienna instinctively deny when he asked his questions? What was going on in their minds? What thought processes brought them to make the statements that they did? Their answers are pure, unprocessed history, the history of a people and a year, 1988.

Winter looked to his own experiences and asked probing questions that shed immense light on the mood of the Viennese fifty years after the Nazi takeover. In his chats at streetcar stops in Vienna, he tapped the nerve of Austrian individual and collective memory. He tickled, he poked, he prodded, he provoked, and the answers he received were at times shocking and at times mundane. The spectrum was broad and surprising. These conversations are documents of the time in which they occurred. They prove that the past is never over. It is always present, and it affects the way we view our surroundings, our environment, our future, and ourselves. The expressions in the photographs and the statements in the conversations show the true feelings of the Viennese fifty years after Austria's annexation by Germany.

Will today's Austrians finally be able to squarely face what happened in 1938 and offer an apology so that they can move forward into the future, or will they continue to avert their gaze from the past? Austria has waited so long to make a gesture that it is now too late for most of those who suffered, but finally, slowly there has been action. It is too late, but nonetheless, the gesture is important. This is what Winter had hoped for, perhaps naïvely, in 1988; it is now a reality for at least a few who are still alive.

Fast Forward: 2008, Vienna—Austrians, especially Viennese, have made progress in facing their common past, but there is still plenty to be done. Only a portion of the crimes committed under the National Socialists have been uncovered. There has been a Historical Commission established and funded by the Republic of Austria that has investigated the transfer and theft of property during the Third Reich, and there is a General Settlement Fund, which has as its objective, to give at least something back to those who had their property stolen or were forced to leave it behind after the German annexation in 1938. But these can only be mere gestures, and some would say that these are only alibis for Austria's politicians and that this will not lead to true closure. This is reflected in the debate about the terms "compensation," "restitution," and "return of property." The events of 1938 cannot be undone. The past is past, but its legacy continues. The dead will not walk again, nor will they be able to live in the houses they were forced to vacate after Austria was annexed by Germany.

Those who fled Austria never received an official apology, since Austria never viewed itself as the legal heir to Hitler's Germany, and when Austrian pangs of conscience did hit, the payments were small. Some buildings are still occupied by the same people who aryanized them in 1938, and Austria's reputation abroad is not helped by vocal populist politicians who seem to have a great deal in common with the Nazis of 1938, at least when their political platforms are compared. Austria as a whole is no longer unrepentant, but certain groups do not make it appear that way.

Is Vienna different now than it was in 1988? Yes, there has been a change. Of those people whom Winter interviewed in 1988, only the younger ones can still be found on the streets today. They are also the ones who most desired a change in attitudes in 1988, and now they hold positions of power. The "war generation" in Austria now consists of old-age pensioners who are slowly dying off, but the impact of the war and their role in it is not forgotten. For better or worse, the Viennese have to live with the echoes of what happened between 1938 and 1945 in their city as part of "Greater Germany." Some still do not see the error of having become part of Hitler's Germany.

Why did Austria finally make this shift? Clearly not because of Austrian openness. It was the result of class-action lawsuits in U.S. courts and bilateral negotiations between U.S. Undersecretary of State Stuart E. Eizenstat and representatives of the Austrian Republic. Eizenstat spearheaded the Clinton Administration's efforts on Holocaust-related issues during Clinton's tenure in office and met with great success.[29] At this time, Austrian banks such as the PSK and Creditanstalt were forced to admit their role in the misuse of Jewish assets during and after the Holocaust, and major Austrian companies must now be very careful about "due diligence," since significant amounts of property and business assets were either transferred or changed hands under the Nazis. Austria is slowly warming to this discussion as those involved pass away. The past is never truly past, but perhaps it can at least be discussed. Time does not heal old wounds; it only covers them until they are properly attended to.

Historians attempt to provide a perspective on these moments in history and a feeling for how it felt to live in Vienna in the period immediately prior to and following March 1938, as well as in 1988, and now in 2008. The real question is how could a city of such art and culture descend into such inhumanity? The Viennese wanted a specific kind of order, and Jews did not fit with that order, whether assimilated or not. With such a viewpoint, it did not seem like inhumanity to the Viennese.

Self-reflection, obviously, can only do so much. Actions, a gesture, an apology, a payment, are needed. These were the promises of Austria's politicians in 1988 but not of many of the Austrian people. In 2008, Vienna remains Vienna, but the people have changed. The younger baby boomers and generation X-ers have moved in. As one former prisoner of war told the writer, "You will not find those people who welcomed the Anschluss on the streets any longer. They are all too old and in failing health."[30]

What he says is true. There were certainly more Viennese of the World War II generation on the streets twenty years ago than there are today. As they slowly pass on, it is easier to talk about the period and what were formerly taboo topics. Despite the positive aspects of this, it is dangerous. There is no longer any corrective to the postwar depiction of this generation as morally corrupt and willing servants of Hitler. This is most certainly not entirely the case. As always, there are gray areas, and the truth lies somewhere in between.

It is the legacy of this generation to have been complicit in Nazi crimes, and it is the legacy of their children and grandchildren to maneuver through the twists and turns of the history surrounding their parents' and grandparents' actions. It is neither an easy task nor an easy legacy, and it will remain so for generations to come. The Viennese remember, but they cannot be sad. They cannot deny their heritage, their parents, their grandparents. The time is right for looking back, but the photographs will still be there on the walls, youthful faces full of energy, wasted in a war for world domination and the destruction of the Jews.

Revisiting Vienna seventy years after the Anschluss, we see that times have changed, but a cloud still hangs over the city. There is a different spirit to this age, but the lives interrupted, altered, and destroyed cannot so simply be righted.

Today, the city has a brochure titled *Jewish Vienna—Heritage and Mission*. In it, Vienna's Mayor Michael Häupl writes, "In cooperation with the Jewish Welcome Service, the City of Vienna thus invites former inhabitants now scattered all over the world to visit—a small symbolic gesture of contemporary Vienna, which posits itself as a city of coexistence, and a modest contribution towards mutual understanding."[31]

There is a gulf between the politicians and the people in what is said and done. The head of Vienna's Jewish community stated quite clearly in a 2007 interview that this is still the case when he said that there is "a huge gap between the official Austria and what people think." For this, he offers a solution: "As long as we sweep everything under the carpet, we will suffer from neuroses; if we confront ourselves with our history, it is no longer a sickness."[32] He is right. The Viennese neurosis continues.

So where do Richard Winter's conversations fit into this Austrian historical picture? Can one classify the people with whom he spoke as "typical" or "average" Austrians? Obviously, a few people cannot speak for an entire nation, but the sentiments expressed in these conversations on the street were definitely a product of the time in which they occurred. The frequent mentions of Austrian President Kurt Waldheim or of Thomas Bernhard's *Heldenplatz* show how preoccupied Austrians were with the events of the day that shed light on their common past. Authors Doron Rabinovici and Gerhard Roth both expressed the sentiment that what began with Waldheim's election is still not entirely finished.[33]

Austria experienced an awakening in 1986 with the Waldheim Affair that continues to this day. The process of confronting the past will continue into the foreseeable future, and the blot of Austrians' role in the Holocaust and in the events of 1938 in Vienna will not be forgotten quickly.

A subject of psychologists for generations to come is the motivation of Austrians to lie about or deny what happened in the past, to whitewash it or improve upon it, to pretend that they do not understand. Still, there is not an accepted answer. It is certainly a coping behavior, but any answer as to the motivation must always be individual. The question of collective versus individual guilt certainly plays a role here, and German philosopher Karl Jaspers put his finger on this early on: You cannot say you are sorry if you are not guilty, but you can be guilty if you do not say that you are sorry. This is the Austrian case.

Saying you are sorry is never easy, but few in Austria who were alive in 1938 even considered that they might have done something wrong. Many were convinced that they needed Hitler, their "rescuer," and blamed Jews for their misery. This brings us to the problem of reality versus feeling in dealing with the past. As illogical as it might seem to glorify Hitler after the events of the Holocaust, there are those who will continue to do so because Hitler helped them by disenfranchising and robbing the Jews. These are the people who still live in aryanized apartments and retired on money earned from aryanized businesses. The Republic of Austria is atoning for their sins and paying their debts.

The conversations in this book clearly show the interaction between individual and collective memory in real life.[34] Individual memory often differs significantly from what collective political memory says is fact. There are political and economic agendas, fear of negative publicity, fear of reprisals or retribution, fear of the truth, but there are also those who personally and privately never wavered in their support for Hitler and the Nazis, and they are the ones who both fascinate and disgust, revolt and repulse us because we cannot comprehend how this is possible. We must delve into the origins of such thoughts and behaviors from the past so that they can be contained and eliminated in the future.

By documenting awkward conversations about the aftermath of the Nazi era, this book seeks to explain the acceptance of propaganda as truth and the denial of truth as propaganda for political ends. This may be only a small contribution to the study of human behavior, but it is nonetheless important, for if we can come to an understanding of why so many people in 1988 refused to accept that what happened in 1938 was a mistake, even after everything was fully known, perhaps we can understand how ordinary citizens can become unfeeling observers or hateful mass murders today and intervene to stop them before it is too late the next time.

Prevention is the best cure for racism, xenophobia, ethnic cleansing, and genocide. If we intervene early enough, perhaps change really is possible. Understanding the genesis of the type of thinking that leads to barbaric behaviors is necessary for change to happen. This book seeks to spur thought about and analyze what has occurred in the aftermath of what remains history's most horrific genocide to date, the Holocaust.

Endnotes

[1] Thomas Weyr, *The Setting of the Pearl: Vienna under Hitler* (New York: Oxford, 2005).

[2] Dokumentationsarchiv des österreichischen Widerstandes (ed.), *Widerstand und Verfolgung in Wien: 1934–1945*, 3 Vols. 2nd ed. (Vienna: ÖBV, 1984), specifically the section in vol. 3 on the persecution of the Jews in Vienna.

[3] For a general history of the Austrian Nazi Party and the events leading up to the Anschluss in English, see Bruce F. Pauley, *Hitler and the Forgotten Nazis: A History of Austrian National Socialism* (Chapel Hill: University of North Carolina Press, 1981), especially Chapter VII: Terror, Counterterror, and Propaganda and Chapter XII: The Execution: Berchtesgaden and the Anschluss.

[4] Ibid.

[5] Historisches Museum der Stadt Wien, *Catalog Wien 1938* (110. Sonderausstellung, 11. März bis 30. Juni 1988, Rathaus Volkshalle).

[6] For further details about the number of Jewish residents of Vienna, see Jonny Moser's statistics from *Demographie der jüdischen Bevölkerung Österreichs 1938–1945* (Vienna: DÖW, 1999) online at www.doew.at/projekte/holocaust/shoahengl/demo2.html; and Raul Hilberg, *The Destruction of the European Jews* (Chicago: Quadrangle Books, 1967). A searchable database of those Austrian Jews murdered during the Holocaust is available at www.doew.at/thema/thema_alt/holocaust/namerfass/engl2.html.

[7] See George Clare, *Last Waltz in Vienna: The Rise and Destruction of a Family, 1842–1942* (New York: Holt, Rinehart and Winston, 1980); and Ruth Kluger, *Still Alive: A Holocaust Girlhood Remembered* (New York: Feminist Press, 2003).

[8] For statistics on Jewish suicides in Vienna, see Gerhard Botz, *Nationalsozialismus in Wien: Machtübernahme und Herrschaftssicherung 1938/39*, 3rd ed. (Buchloe: dvo, 1988), especially pages 99–105.

[9] Botz, 101.

[10] Botz, 103.

[11] Franz Theodor Csokor, *Auch heute noch nicht an Land: Briefe und Gedichte aus dem Exil* (Vienna: Ephelant, 1993).

[12] "Nachrede. Umfrage. Wegbegleiter und Kritiker über Kurt Waldheim," *profil* 25, 18 June 2007, 26.

[13] Herbert Lackner, "Pflicht und Dunke," *profil* 25, 18 June 2007, 22, 24.

[14] For a documentation put together by supporters of Waldheim about his biography in English, see *Kurt Waldheim's Wartime Years: A Documentation* (Vienna: Carl Gerold's Sohn Verlagsbuchhandlung K.G., 1987).

[15] Thomas Bernhard, "Heldenplatz," *Conjunctions* (Bard College) 33 (Fall 1999): 307–408.

[16] Christine Kiebuzinska, "The Scandal Maker: Thomas Bernhard and the Reception of *Heldenplatz,*" *Modern Drama* 38(3) (Fall 1995): 378–388. For a history of the play and selected press reviews, see Jens Dittmar, ed., *Thomas Bernhard Werksgeschichte* (Frankfurt a.M.: Suhrkamp, 1990), 330–337.

[17] Gustav Spann and Peter Malina, *1938 1988* (Vienna: BMWK, 1988).

[18] Ruth Kluger, *Still Alive: A Holocaust Girlhood Remembered* (New York: Feminist Press, 2003), 26.

[19] Günter Bischof, "Victims? Perpetrators? 'Punching Bags' of European Historical Memory? The Austrians and Their World War II Legacies," *German Studies Review* 27(1) 2004: 17–32, here 22–23.

[20] The original text of the Moscow Declaration is available online at http://www.yale.edu/lawweb/avalon/wwii/moscow.htm.

[21] Alexander and Margarete Mitscherlich, *The Inability to Mourn: Principles of Collective Behavior,* trans. Beverley R. Placzek (New York: Grove Press, 1975). (Originally published in German as *Die Unfähigkeit zu trauern. Grundlagen kollektiven Verhaltens* by R. Piper & Co. Verlag, Munich, 1967).

[22] For a discussion of this, please consult Peter Sichrovsky, *Born Guilty: Children of Nazi Families,* trans. Jean Steinberg (New York: Basic Books, 1988).

[23] Günther Grass, *The Tin Drum* (New York: Vintage, 1990).

[24] Sichrovsky, 13.

[25] Robert Knight, "Contours of Memory in Post-Nazi Austria," *Patterns of Prejudice* 34(4) 2000: 5–11.

[26] For details on property theft and restitution issues, see Verena Pawlowsky and Harald Wendelin, eds. *Ausgeschlossen und entrechtet. Raub und Rückgabe-Österreich von 1938 bis heute* (Vienna: Mandelbaum, 2006).

[27] Philip Zimbardo, *The Lucifer Effect: How Good People Turn Evil* (London: Rider, 2007), preface, vii, and viii.

[28] Claudia Dreifus, "Finding Hope in Knowing the Universal Capacity for Evil: A Conversation with Philip G. Zimbardo," *New York Times,* 3 April 2007.

[29] Stuart E. Eizenstat, *Imperfect Justice: Looted Assets, Slave Labor, and the Unfinished Business of World War II* (New York: Public Affairs, 2003).

[30] Interview with Horst Leonhard, born 1923, March 2007.

[31] Vienna City Administration, Municipal Department 53—Press and Information Services. *Jewish Vienna—Heritage and Mission* (Vienna: no date. [2007]), 3.

[32] Renate Graber, Interview with Ariel Muzicant, "Wir wollen keine perfekte Welt," *Der Standard,* 7 April 2007, 20 (author's translation).

[33] "Nachrede. Umfrage. Wegbegleiter und Kritiker über Kurt Waldheim," *profil* 25, 18 June 2007, 26.

[34] For a discussion of collective versus individual guilt, see Karl Jaspers, *The Question of German Guilt* (Fourth Impression), trans. E. B. Ashton (New York: Capricorn Books, 1961), in which Jaspers argues that there cannot be collective guilt, only individual guilt.

For two days, I decided to let Vienna's elegance and charm enchant me. I was there alone on assignment for the *New York Times Magazine* to write about Vienna's burst of creativity at the turn of the twentieth century.

For those two days, I let myself be dazzled by the city as a tourist might. The old city pulled me back to the great days of the Habsburg Empire, and the music of Mozart floated above the mochas and strudels in the coffeehouses. The *Ringstrasse* led me to the ornate Opera House where I scored a ticket to Figaro, and the next evening I entered the dark red *Musikverein*, home of Philharmonic Concert Hall and of Universal Editions, the classical music publisher, for a chamber music concert. I gawked at historical Heldenplatz—the plaza of heroes—and admired the gold and white Secession Museum built at the turn of the twentieth century when renegade geniuses like Klimt and Schiele and Freud and Mahler were inventing modernism.

I'd willed myself to forget for those two days that those geniuses were made miserable by the Viennese establishment or that Schubert went hungry or that Mozart was buried in a pauper's grave. Or that in 1938, Vienna watched and often cheered as its Jews—10 percent of its population—were being humiliated, spat upon, and exterminated if they did not escape in time.

Vienna's ironies can be disorienting. For example, the birthplace of psychoanalysis is a city embroiled in an elaborate pattern of denial and revisionism. These shadows are hard for a visitor to imagine while walking around that glittering town and even harder for the Viennese themselves to acknowledge.

On the third day of my visit, my late husband, Richard Winter, flew in from New York. The persistent dark side of Vienna was by no means forgettable to Ricki who, at age seventeen in 1938, finally managed to flee German-occupied Vienna, having been sent back twice when his escape routes were closed, although he'd signed a declaration that he would not return at the risk of being sent to a concentration camp.

Evan Burr Bukey in *Hitler's Austria* describes what went on "on March 11, 1938, when Vienna prepared to receive Hitler . . . untold thousands of Viennese took to the streets of their city like madpersons, dragging anyone who 'looked Jewish' from vehicles, clubbing and beating victims, desecrating synagogues, robbing department stores, and raiding Jewish apartments. They compelled rabbis to scrub toilet bowls with prayer shawls and stole whatever cash, jewelry, and furs they could find. An SS correspondent would later write admiringly, 'The Viennese have managed to do overnight what we have failed to achieve in the slow-moving, ponderous north up to this day. In Austria, a boycott of the Jews does not need organizing. The people themselves have initiated it.'"[1]

Bukey continues, "This horror was a prelude to what would occur in Vienna *and* in Austria's provincial cities during the *Kristallnacht.* Statistics for November 9–10, a nightmare period not easily matched in previous European history, include 267 synagogues destroyed, 7,500 businesses and homes devastated, 91 Jews murdered, and 26,000 Jews rounded up."[2]

Many Viennese admit with an odd combination of coyness and resignation that beneath their city's ornate surface—the wreath of Renaissance and baroque imperial buildings on the Ringstrasse surrounding the old city, the prancing *Lippizzaners*, the unsurpassed opera, chamber and orchestral music, countless museums—lies an equally intense darkness.

As Richard Winter's photographs and conversations in this book reflect, there is not much self scrutiny in the city where Freud mapped the unconscious.

Historian David Luft pinned down Freud's significance above and beyond the specifics of psychoanalysis in *Eros and Inwardness in Vienna.* "Freud's intellectual significance lies not so much in the details of his theory or of his scientific method as in his general approach to human nature: his emphasis on the enormous role that psychological matters play in human behavior and suffering, and his development of the notion of a talking method within a human relationship as a means of cure by love."[3]

On the fiftieth anniversary of Freud's death, according to Thomas Smolka, treasurer of the Sigmund Freud Gesellschaft, the Conservative Party protested naming a street after him on behalf of nearby residents who objected to having "Freud" in their address. The mayor resolved the conflict by designating an area near the famous Votiv Church "Sigmund Freud Park," ensuring that the address change would be unnecessary.

Yet in 1988, an advertising campaign abroad featured Freud's beautiful great-granddaughter sitting in a coffeehouse with the slogan: "Come to Vienna!" an appeal to his popularity abroad designed to lure tourists. A fifty-schilling note bore Freud's picture, and so did postage stamps, but there was little sign of the influence of the Sigmund Freud who probed the surface to reveal what it hides. His old apartment is maintained for tourists as a museum by the Freud Society; but the Freud Museum, which houses his famous couch, is located in London. What a field day Freud might have had—if his heart did not break—with the fact that Austria commemorated the centennial of his birth with an exhibit of couches by contemporary Austrian furniture designers.

After tourists are bused past the Sigmund Freud Park, they visit a shop where they can buy *Mozartkugeln*—little chocolates wrapped in foil bearing Mozart's picture. An ad campaign for Austrian Airlines didn't flaunt its astonishingly superb service, but instead featured huge photographs of Mozart playing the piano and pouring champagne. The Habsburg era and the turn of the twentieth century and the Nazi time have been turned into settings for sitcoms and movies and computer games.

On March 13, as Hitler's troops marched into Vienna to the tune of the "*Horst Wessel Lied*," Ricki Winter, a six-foot-four seventeen year old was struggling to look inconspicuous inside a movie theater, and, as he heard the music, he responded viscerally with pleasure. His foot tapped, his spirit even rose for a moment before he caught himself. After all, this was his music, his patriotism that was somehow being distorted into his death knell.

His family was deeply Austrian. His uncles had fought in the First World War, his father was the CEO of Universal Editions, the largest music publishing house in the world with offices in the grand Philharmonic Hall. His family's apartment on the *Nussdorferstrasse* was next door to the house where Franz Schubert had lived.

After we were married, he'd bring me with him every year to Vienna to go to concerts, the opera, the *Heurigen*, and on hikes in the *Wienerwald*, and to spend time with his beloved Tante Nelly, who (unlike most of his relatives, who were murdered) had miraculously survived the

Holocaust, hidden with her husband in the attic of a heroic Catholic
family. She had been in her early forties when the war started, older than
I was when I met her.

Visiting Nelly was like going back to the nineteenth century—the
Biedermeier furniture, the low ceilings and small rooms, oil paintings
in wide gilt frames, fresh roses from her formal garden arranged in
crystal vases—and Nelly, in the center of it all with her lioness's mane
of hair brushed turn-of-the-century high around her head, in her bold
black-and-purple dress and pearls. Nelly lived in what could be almost
described as a time warp; she had not been into the center of her own
city since before the Nazis came. I tried very hard to persuade her to
come to the opera with us or just to ride around the Ringstrasse, but
she refused. She preferred to remember it and her life there the way it
had once been for her. Sometimes she and Alyce Winter, Ricki's other
aunt who had survived the Nazis, would visit one another for coffee and
conversation.

Nelly was as regal and warm a woman as I've ever met. After our
first lunch together, while my husband napped as he had as a boy on her
chaise plumped with huge embroidered pillows, she talked to me in her
old-fashioned, high-pitched combination of German and English and
French. Widening her eyes for emphasis, she told me what a wonderful
little boy my husband had been—he could have been an Olympic skater,
she was sure. Then she went on to describe the sadism she'd endured
in war-time Vienna shortly after her husband died. Under Nazi law,
Nelly—a Jew—had been shielded because her husband was Protestant;
without this protection, she was declared an "enemy of the people." She
told me about the ordeal that followed, introducing each detail slowly
and with some difficulty, ending by saying that for three years she never
saw the light of day.

Aunt Nelly and Susan Winter Balk

After we had talked for several hours, Nelly gave me two gifts.
First, she opened the top drawer of her ornate baroque dresser and took
out a long strand of tiny pearls. Then I watched her walk over to her
Biedermeier closet and reach up high to a shelf for something that was
flat and wrapped in tissue paper. She nodded for me to come take it. I
imagined a brocade shawl, but I was wrong. Inside the package was a
folded piece of rough orange fabric stamped with rows and rows of six-
pointed stars—the word "Jude" printed inside each star—an uncut sheet
of cloth badges that the Nazis once forced all Jews to wear as their marks.

I reeled for a moment from the eeriness of what I saw, from the contrast between the lush mosaic of her salon and the brute truth of her gift. I can still see the almost maternal look on her face as she watched me remove the tissue paper. I can still see my husband sitting on that curl-backed chaise after his nap, staring blankly at the Nazi cloth he held between his fingers, the way I'd seen him hold the fashionable textiles he designed back in New York City. I knew then that I was a member of the family.

I wear Nelly's pearls almost every day; but I still don't know what to do with the terrifying fabric, so I keep it on a shelf in my closet, and almost every morning as I get dressed I look at it for a moment—it's hard for me to say why.

In summers, the family moved to their home in Heidenreichstein where his mother's family owned a metalworks factory, Bruder Eisert. He took me with him to Heidenreichstein and showed me where he'd gone swimming, played tennis, and picked mushrooms, and measured the flow and the depth of the river from season to season. We toured the factory and the local castle and visited a man he remembered from his childhood. One elderly man greeted him warmly and said rather emotionally that the way his family and other Jews had been treated had been disgraceful.

Richard Winter and Aunt Alyce

He had returned to Vienna dozens of times for pleasure by the time we met at a Greenwich Village art gallery in 1975. But—perhaps inspired by the old man from Heidenreichstein—in 1988, he returned for just one reason: to ask a cross-section of Viennese, mostly random strangers, about their thoughts and feelings towards and memories of the Nazi era.

He went to tram stops and talked to waiting passengers. First, he introduced himself and explained that he was a journalist doing research; then he asked if the person was from Austria. If so, he asked what he or she was most proud of about Austria. He listened and either gave follow-up questions to the answers or else proceeded to ask what that person thought about what went on during the time of the Nazi occupation of Austria. Most of the time he asked to take the person's photograph. He often asked follow-up questions, always very interested in people's opinions.

We met at the end of the workday to have dinner together and compare the results of our research. I know he was very serious about his work and respectful of the people he interviewed. He found what most of them said fascinating professionally, even if personally he was disappointed by some of the answers.

He was not naïve, but it was hard for him to imagine that people would deliberately have taken Vienna from him rather than simply have shared it with him.

Although he'd lived in America for thirty-six years when we met in 1975, he taught me to sing "*Wien, Wien, Nur Du Allein*" on our second date, and we swooned together to Schubert's quintets.

Ricki (he always insisted on being called by his Viennese nickname, which was not always easy for Americans talking to a six-foot-four grown man) loved his life in America and he thrived in America, but, until he died at eighty in 2000, half of his heart was Viennese.

He was full of stories of Bruno Walter, Igor Stravinsky, Alban Berg, Alma Mahler, Kurt Weill, and Anton Webern, whom he had known through his father. He kept a framed photograph of his father in his office with Igor Stravinsky in the living room where chamber music recordings almost always played in the background.

In that living room, I often heard heated but witty arguments about the character of the Viennese, great jokes about Count Rudi and Count

Igor Stravinsky and Hugo Winter at Universal Editions

Bobi, and wonderful firsthand anecdotes about Vienna before the war from Ricki and his closest friends—other Jewish Viennese refugees— Reserl Peterson whom he called his "great Platonic love," whom he'd met standing in line at the American Embassy in 1938 waiting to get visas; Serge Sabarsky, the Klimt and Schiele art dealer whose personal collection, along with that of Ronald Lauder, became the permanent

Serge Sabarsky

collection of New York's Neue Galerie; the psychoanalyst Hannah Kapit; and the fashion designer Helga Howie.

On one trip to Europe, we traveled with a close young American friend, Scott Ciabattari, who, after hearing countless stories, was eager to see Ricki's Vienna firsthand. As the train from Italy moved up through southern Austria, Ricki talked about politics, explaining the then-growing popularity of the neo-fascist politician, Jöerg Haider.

"I'm confused, Rick," Scott said impatiently. "Do you love this place or not?"

After a long pause came the answer: "You understand perfectly. You've been listening very, very carefully."

"You mean you don't know the answer either?"

Ricki just smiled. Scott shook his head, also smiling.

"If you're confused now," I told him, "wait until we get to Vienna!"

The first night in Vienna, we met our good friend, Tom Smolka, at

Richard Winter and Reserl Peterson at a Viennese winery

the Schwarzenberg Café on the Schwarzenbergplatz. Tom's Viennese Jewish parents had moved to England in 1933, and then returned to Vienna when Tom was ten, right after the war.

They loved to tell stories, and they loved to argue. A favorite story that Tom told for Scott's benefit was this:

> There's a ruckus on a streetcar, and a lady asks what the problem is.
> "It's all the fault of the Jews and the bicycle riders," the driver shoots back.
> "Why the bicycle riders?" asks the lady.
> An old man in the middle of the bus looks up from his book. "Why the Jews?"

Tom and Ricki had a running disagreement about the Viennese. "You're a romantic, my dear Ricki," Tom would say lovingly.

"You lived in Austria before the war in your youth so you're blinded by golden memories. I lived here after the war, and to me there's no romance at all. It's simple. In Vienna, tens of thousands of people wanted nicer apartments, and they got nicer apartments when the Jews disappeared, so what is there for them to regret?"

"But they must on some level know it was wrong," Ricki would argue.

Tom would shake his head and smile warmly. "You're confusing them with the Germans. In Germany there was a bit of re-education after the war. In Austria there was absolutely none. In schools all the way until 1988, nothing was taught about what happened from 1934 on, so nobody had the feeling that anything was amiss!"

Tom would then draw from his experiences running his family's ski-binding business Tyrolia, which was taken over by a Nazi during the war. When he fled after the war, the family got it back by court order.

One day a customer walked into my office saying, "I never do business with Jews, but you're an exception," whereupon Tom told him he wouldn't do business with this Jew either and escorted him out of the building.

In 1988, Ricki—an American citizen for forty-nine years—received notice that the Austrian government was offering him, as a refugee, the opportunity to apply for "a onetime financial grant." If he qualified—that is, if he had to emigrate in order to escape persecution and was now in financial distress (with an income that did not exceed $732 a month!)—he might be eligible for a maximum of $476. He laughed and threw the letter away.

A few years later, he received a questionnaire that indicated if he answered it correctly, he would qualify for two thousand dollars for "pain and suffering."

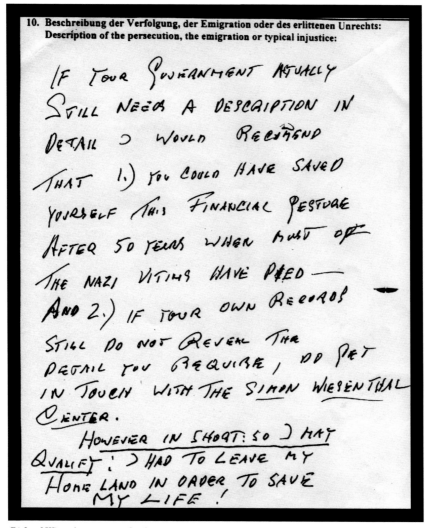

10. Beschreibung der Verfolgung, der Emigration oder des erlittenen Unrechts:
Description of the persecution, the emigration or typical injustice:

IF YOUR GOVERNMENT ACTUALLY STILL NEED A DESCRIPTION IN DETAIL I WOULD RECOMEND THAT 1.) YOU COULD HAVE SAVED YOURSELF THIS FINANCIAL GESTURE AFTER 50 YEARS WHEN MOST OF THE NAZI VITIMS HAVE DIED — AND 2.) IF YOUR OWN RECORDS STILL DO NOT REVEAL THE DETAIL YOU REQUIRE, DO GET IN TOUCH WITH THE SIMON WIESENTHAL CENTER. HOWEVER IN SHORT: SO I MAY QUALIFY: I HAD TO LEAVE MY HOME LAND IN ORDER TO SAVE MY LIFE!

Richard Winter's response to the Austrian government's questionnaire

Unlike West Germany, where there has been a continued, substantial effort to come to terms with the Nazi era (and the government has paid huge restitutions to its victims), the history curriculum in Austrian public schools had not, until 1986, included any significant coverage of that period. Since most parents and grandparents hardly ever talked to their children about it, many young adults had been unaware of what occurred in their city just a half a century before.

Elfriede Jelinek, the 2004 Nobel Prize winner, in her 1980 novel, *Wonderful, Wonderful Times*, traces how Nazism was transmitted to the children of Nazis. "In post-war Germany, the crimes were worked through, letter by letter," says Jelinek. "But in Austria, because we wanted to be viewed positively by the Allies, we needed to deny our complicity with the Nazis and portray ourselves as 'little innocents.' One mustn't forget that Hitler learnt his anti-Semitism from trashy magazines in Austria and was exported to Germany as a complete political mind. Anti-Semitism was once our great export, so to speak."[4]

Many Austrians resented the fact that their president, Kurt Waldheim, was included on the list of Nazis barred from the United States. Few were outraged by Waldheim's involvement with Nazi activities (exposed primarily by non-Austrian newspapers) or by his sanctimonious stance once his history as a senior Nazi involved in sending Greek Jews to concentration camps had been revealed. Viennese newspaper editorials repeated week after week: Our president is our business; this is not the business of foreigners, *Ausländern*.

Ausländer is a term of exclusion used to refer matter-of-factly even to citizens of Austria with non-Austrian last names, people with dark skin, or minorities of any kind. There is little effort made to mask the derision.

There's no question that anti-Semitism endures in Vienna. When conductor Lorin Maazel began his tenure as director of the Vienna State Opera, hundreds of flyers floated down from the balconies reading "Go home, Jew!" And some Viennese who are Jewish or of Jewish descent, because they're part of a community that is uncomfortable with the subject of Jews, are themselves uneasy with it.

Some of our Viennese relatives were born in England after their parents had escaped from Vienna, and moved back to Austria after the war. Many of them refer to Jews as "them." One is a beautiful woman, a physician and an intellectual. A few years ago, her twelve-year-old daughter asked my husband: "Are you Protestant or Catholic?" He replied, "I'm Jewish." When the girl asked, "What's Jewish?" her mother said quickly, "Don't you remember—I told you, my parents were Jewish!" The girl did not remember.

Friedensreich Hundertwasser, the popular Viennese painter and environmentalist who himself was half-Jewish, told me in his glass atelier across from the Imperial Palace in 1987 that he believes there was an "international mafia out to discredit Waldheim."

Yet there are exceptions to this pattern of denial and belated approbation. Hubertus Czernin, a political editor of the weekly magazine *Profil*, broke the stories of Waldheim's Nazi record.

A small but vehement group fought a ground swell of public and official opposition and managed to erect a monument to the Holocaust near the opera house. In 1988, sculptor Alfred Hrdlicka's still controversial memorial was unveiled. The monument consists of marble columns portraying the gates of hell, and, dwarfed between them, a dark metal figure of an old, bearded Jewish man on his hands and knees, scrubbing the street.

A non-Jewish friend of ours who was active in the campaign against Waldheim believes the memorial is appropriate. "Many Austrians say they did not know of the extermination of the Jews, but there is no one who was here in 1938 who does not remember seeing an old man forced to scrub the street to remove propaganda signs opposing the Nazi Party."

And yet because there is no plaque to identify the man as a Jew, there's no way for the uninitiated to understand what they're passing as they stroll by. Often people would stop and sit on the old man's back to eat their lunch, with no idea of what the sculpture represents. So barbed wire (barbed wire!) was later installed on the back of the street-scrubber to keep the strollers from lounging on his back.

One Friday night in 1988, my husband and I had a dinner date a block from the opera house with an old friend, Litzy Berner, who had been heroic in the underground as a young woman. I arranged to join them half an hour late so I could walk over at sundown and put a couple of pebbles on the monument to that old man on his hands and

Richard Winter in his darkroom

knees—the old Jewish tradition of showing respect at a grave. "Why?" my husband asked when I joined them. "You're not such a religious person."

"Because no one remembers them," I told him.

"Believe me, I remember them," he said.

"*So do I*," said Litzy, and she squeezed my hand.

"I know you remember them," I said, thinking of Artur and Erwin, Ricki's twin uncles whose ashes his then-forty-year-old father had been called to collect from a train station from a matter-of-fact bureaucrat one summer afternoon in 1938.

All three of us were quiet for a few minutes, lost in what we remembered. Then we raised our glasses, and my husband gave the toast he repeated every time he drank a glass of wine: "To love and friendship!"

How my husband loved the city he fled!

Perhaps naively, he believed that if Viennese looked at the truth about the Nazi era fifty years afterward, they'd be horrified. And then apologetic on behalf of the perpetrators of the genocide.

But unmarked memorials won't unlock the amnesia. Putting pebbles on a statue or driving past a park named after Freud won't bring enlightenment about what led to the Holocaust.

Richard Winter's hope was that these face-to-face conversations would demystify the horrors of the past for him. He never came to terms with the cruelties of the Nazi time, and neither did most of the people with whom he spoke.

He wanted this book to show the reasons for his passionate ambivalence, to demystify the persistent pathology of hate and murder and denial and to strengthen our understanding so that a horror such as the one his Vienna had endured might be less likely to visit the world again.

Endnotes

1. Evan Burr Bukey. *Hitler's Austria: Popular Sentiment in the Nazi Era, 1938–1945* (Chapel Hill: University of North Carolina Press. 2000), 134.
2. Bukey, 144.
3. David S. Luft, *Eros and Inwardness in Vienna: Weininger, Musil, Doderer* (Chicago: University of Chicago Press, 2003), p. 6.
4. Elfrieda Jelenik, *Wonderful, Wonderful Times*, translation of *Die Ausgesperrten* by Michael Hulse (London: Serpent's Tale, 1990).

In the fall of 1988, exactly half a century after escaping from Nazi Vienna, I returned with my camera. I photographed everything I saw—people in as many places as possible. I tried to see everything—soccer games, flea markets, fancy parties, subways, trolleys, offices. The faces in each of these settings convinced me, as the great German photographer August Sander insisted, that "peoples' character is etched into their faces."

Many of these Austrian faces reflect the ravages of guilt. Since Austria had maintained for fifty years that it was the innocent victim of the Nazi invasion, Austrians—typified by Kurt Waldheim—had never faced up to their responsibility for the atrocities committed during that time. I was curious about how they might have come to terms with their collective past, so I began interviewing many of the same people I photographed. In their voices, I very often heard the guarded discomfort of amnesia.

The fall of 1988 was a unique moment for Austria because the fiftieth anniversary of the Anschluss was being commemorated. For the first time, Austria was acknowledging what had been officially denied for fifty years. Even Walter Cronkite, host of the annual New Year's concert by the Vienna Philharmonic, had offhandedly referred to the Nazi years as "the time when Austria disappeared from the map."

Nothing about the Nazis was taught in the public schools, unless individual teachers initiated such a lesson. And there was a controversy brewing about a memorial to the slaughtered Jews, which was to be erected in the middle of Vienna. Many people preferred not to flaunt what they felt was unnecessary unpleasantness.

So the work presented here was done against a background of several controversies, which I systematically referred to in questions to my subjects:

1. March 1988 marked fifty years since Hitler and his forces officially made Austria part of Germany, an event that caused tens of thousands of Austrians to gather at the *Heldenplatz* (Heroes' Square) in Vienna to greet Hitler in a frenzy of joyous adoration.

2. Austria had recently elected Kurt Waldheim its new president, in spite of incriminating material linkage to Nazi crimes uncovered during his campaign, when his signed initials were found on documents deporting thousands of Jews and Greeks—many to their deaths. His election had been vehemently challenged by many socialists, the foreign press, and the United Jewish Congress.

3. Most importantly, Austrian officials, in the face of the very negative foreign press that continued to bring to light Austria's role in the Second World War, decided to use the occasion of the fiftieth anniversary of its annexation to Germany to finally tell the truth to her own people. The truth turned out to be very different from Waldheim's widely publicized statement of 1986, which had proclaimed: "This fine people of seven million, who never caused any disturbance in the world, can walk into the future in a spirit of general solidarity and brotherhood."

A very strong and well-organized re-education campaign took place. Almost daily, the media and special events showed and discussed what Austria's participation in the Nazi horror actually had been. Much of the younger audiences were perplexed. All of Austria was suddenly told that she was not the helpless victim as they had heard for most of their lives from their elders. Instead, Austria was a more-than-willing participant in the Nazi crimes.

Surprisingly, very little was done to celebrate or honor the heroes of the resistance, which might have allowed the people to have a positive rallying point. Therefore, many Austrians became angry and overwhelmed. They saw this important national exercise—called the *aufarbeiten* or "working through" and getting in touch with their past so they could move toward a clear, healthier future—as a betrayal by its own officials, a belated effort to portray them as collectively guilty.

4. At the same time, a play by Austria's most famous playwright, Thomas Bernhard, was about to open on the grand occasion of

the one hundredth anniversary of the most distinguished Vienna Burgtheater. The name of the play, *Heldenplatz*, was the site of the 1939 frenzied welcome to Hitler.

Huge controversy had arisen over the staging, action, dialogue, and title of the play. Parts of the dialogue of the play had just been leaked to the press. This created fierce oppositions and wide demands that the play not be allowed to be performed, with the opposition in daily debate from sessions of the Austrian parliament to the most extreme articles in the *Kronenzeitung*, Austria's largest newspaper, because the play violently and dramatically attacked Austria's national character.

As I systematically brought up each of these controversial events, I tried to capture the reactions both on the faces and in the words of my subjects. Not all of them agreed to be interviewed. And some I was unable to photograph. Also, I decided not to use flash or strobe lights for the sake of spontaneity, which explains why some of the photographs have a grainy texture.

—Richard Winter

One afternoon in a streetcar terminal, I approached a man and asked him how he felt about Austria's responsibility for the Nazi horror. He responded:

I'm a religious guy. I believe in divine providence. What God and the angels want to do is none of our business. God wanted Hitler to become Reich chancellor, and God made the Second World War happen.

Suddenly a woman sitting close by waiting for a streetcar interrupts angrily.

Why don't you work on your Negro problems? A saying goes "everybody should sweep in front of his own door," understand? You have to think about the Indians in America, about the blacks. That's exactly the same that we did to the Jews. I have to LAUGH that you come here to ask us questions about our extermination camps.

Do you find it okay that the Austrians exterminated Jews?

I do not find it okay that you are trying to play the role of judge here. You have you own problems with the Indians and Negros, no?

The woman walks away angrily. I approach a young man who introduces himself as a medical student who stands nearby and ask him why he thinks the woman was so hostile and evasive.

It comes directly from the subconscious; you can't touch these people. I am interested in talking about our recent past, but very few Austrians are willing to talk with me.

I am very atypical, but it's very hard to guess at what percentage of Austrians I represent, since everybody is quiet. I'm lucky since I've had a longer period of education than most people. In school, I always studied history. I visited the Austrian concentration camp Mathausen, so I have a great deal of information of what went on. But other people know absolutely nothing. If you speak to neo-Nazi people, who are still Nazis today, they have no idea what went on. They don't know about concentration camps; they deny it and push it away.

I do not condemn anybody who was once a Nazi. The Nazi part was simply an organization of thought, a political movement which today at the age of forty, I really cannot condemn.

I wouldn't tell anybody that he or she should have been in the resistance. Some of our young people today talk this way. It is very nervy to do this. Also, it is the haughty pretentiousness of youth.

General Secretary Heide Schmidt of the right wing Freedom Party about the Freedom Party view looking back to the Nazi time.

Now you can't tell anybody you were in the war—the young people are too stupid to understand. The young ones have it good now, and everybody says, "You were so stupid, why did you serve?" You can't talk to the young people.

How do you think Austria should be viewed abroad?

I'd like it to be viewed as the country of Mozart and the Alps, and Mozart candy, but it is not.

The Austrians themselves.

They don't have a good image. Not a very good picture abroad.

And how is it with your parents and your grandparents. The connection to the Nazi time? Are there troubles?

It's not discussed.

But on the other hand you accept one another. And it's just not discussed. And that works?

Yes. You just leave it alone.

And that works?

Yes, it works.

Looking back on the Nazi era, do you think that enough has been done? Is there still past left to be dealt with?

There's not enough dealing with the past, for sure. I'm still pacified too often. That's at least my impression. I think it was a lot worse than they say.

What was the worst thing for Austria about the Nazi era?

Good question. The whole thing. The worst was that our fathers and mothers believed it too.

The Viennese were pretty evil anti-Semites. Do you believe that or do you think that it wasn't as bad as everybody says?

It was certainly, like people say, it was worse. There's no doubt about that.

The young, they say: "Why were you so stupid?" We had to. If you had said no, you'd have been shot instantly.

They know that too.

They don't. They are too stupid to know. Today, our generation, the postwar problems that we had; we rebuilt Vienna. The young are better off and everybody asks, why we were that stupid. Why did you go? The young can't say.

Do you think that the Nazi time has been dealt with?

I don't care.

During the last two years, part of the population has unfortunately again more and more begun to demonstrate this really "*miese Oesterreichische Volksseele*" (despicable Austrian soul) which always existed, and now have re-erupted to new heights with the Waldheim affair.

One notices here "*Einen miesen Kleinbeuergerlichen*" instinct (a despicable small-minded instinct), the virulent articulation of which is steadily growing with strong support of the newspaper *Kronenzeitung*, the most popular paper in Vienna and Austria.

This is the voice of inhumanity and intolerance which, if it were possible, would like all those who could be potentially critical to their views be banned from Austria. These tendencies go from the Second World War generation, unfortunately too often, all the way to our youth of today. Only yesterday a functionary of the *Oesterreichische Volkspartei* (Austrian People's Party) told me that he had to justify himself before a meeting of a "*Mittelschüler Kartell Verein*" (High School Youth Forum) because his party had placed an ad in the paper of the *Kultusgemeinde* congratulating the Jews on the occasion of their New Year. These kinds of incidents should not be generalized. However, they are indicators that prove "*Es Weht ein Übler Geist durch Deses Land.*"

Hubertus Czernin, founding publisher of Profil, *the Austrian magazine which was the first to expose Waldheim's Nazi past in the country.*

I don't know why America (American press) is now attacking Austria so much. I don't understand it.

I'm proud of the culture and the people and the president of the Republic of Austria, whom I personally know. He was unfortunately attacked in a way that he didn't disserve. I know him from my youth. He was not a Nazi. It is all the fault of the U.S.A., because after the First World War, the whole world and your president helped disseminate Europe. That was the beginning and why National Socialism has come to power. Then nobody stopped Hitler, and now the war was little Austria's fault? Now they call Germany and Austria countries of criminals. It's ridiculous.

America has lost a lot with me, with its Waldheim story.

The difficulty about your president is that not only the 1930s and '40s and the Nazi era, where there was so much "horror," is connected with terrible events, but that Dr. Waldheim wore an SS uniform.

I have a counter question.

Sure.

Let's look at it the other way around. Say it didn't happen in Germany and Austria, let's move it to America. Don't you think that in this case exactly the same number of people would have joined the SS? With the old ideologies, which were in the beginning early history of Austria. After all, Waldheim was very young back then.

Could it have happened in the United States like here? I don't think so.

The clientele consists mostly of artists and intellectuals, and I'd say 90 percent of us are against anti-Semitism and were against the election of Kurt Waldheim.

The way I see it, there are two Austrias—the one that elected Waldheim, and the Austria that you see here which did not.

The commemoration of the fiftieth anniversary of the Nazi annexation caused a good airing out of our past, and I believe the moral hygiene here improved a bit. But at the same time, the anti-Semitism became more articulated. This confrontation has brought it out of hiding.

I was never in America, but I am deeply interested in Austria's recent history and how it's reported in America. The public over there has not the faintest idea what took place. They know even less than the Austrian public, which is saying a lot; and now after fifty years, suddenly there is an explosion of information about what happened there.

The international powers are really responsible for what happened here. They will call you a good guy if you have millions of dollars, and they will decorate you no matter what you said or did. Otherwise, as with Waldheim, they suddenly find out after fifty years that you are absolutely rotten.

A real denazification never took place here, the reasons for which I very much dislike talking about.

From the first hour on, there has been tremendous corruption among what we called "professional antifascists." The government had been dependent on the old Nazi officeholders who were naturally delighted to be allowed to continue in their highly rewarding offices and slowly managed to get old buddies back in.

Two gentlemen in a coffeehouse (Josefstädter Street):

Man one, the director of an insurance company:

For me as a middle-European it is incomprehensible how this Waldheim business got stirred up outside of Austria. Why try to force a negative view of things? Why not try to look positively at the future? And why unearth things which are now so long ago? Why try to shovel last year's snow?

And your media not only says Waldheim lied but says all Austrians are liars. And when you say that Waldheim wore the SS uniform—couldn't that just as easily have happened in America?

Man two:

I do not believe *Heldenplatz* should be permitted to be performed. Bernhard's characters are silly. Believe me, I know a lot of Jews, and they are all much too elegant to express themselves in the exaggerated and aggressive way Bernhard portrays them.

An art historian, friend of playwright Thomas Bernhard:

Austria probably has the worst German-speaking press in the world. On the other hand, we probably have the world's best German-speaking writers and poets—almost all of whom are virulently critical of their countrymen, society, and politics.

Two retired district attorneys at a coffeehouse (Josefstädter Street) about the play Heldenplatz*:*

Man one:

This aggressively self-accusing play that throws stones at our own people should not come to be performed now, when these matters have been overly played up anyway and are finally over with. Why start up again?

Man two about Austrian hostilities to foreigners residing there:

America is at fault in all this. They took the experts from us and left the others. Naturally, this caused a large amount of hate, and for that hate, the United States is to blame.

Man two:

All this reexamination and reevaluation is bad. It was not a good idea to bring this to light now. Anti-Semitism, which had been quiet for a while, became virulent again through these endless examinations. Everything had been forgotten. What's the point of bringing it all up again?

Man one about the supposed unawareness of the general public of the Nazi horrors:

In '41 in Poland, my commanding officers and I went for a walk, and we saw a group of people standing in the icy cold. I asked my commanding officer what they were doing there, and the man who was otherwise a charming and warm person shouted out to me, "Keep your mouth shut. You don't know anything about this." So naturally, I kept my mouth shut till after the war.

As an Upper Austrian I had to live through that experience. My father was a simple laborer, and when Hitler marched in, he said that one shouldn't witness that.

One shouldn't witness that? What does that mean?

Well, if Austria goes down. In opposition to maybe Vienna, on the Heldenplatz. Well, I was there, in Upper Austria, and Hitler was from Upper Austria, so were the circles of the religious and the followers of the Habsburgs who didn't let Hitler convince them. They weren't convinced either.

Ha, ha. Reparations, you don't know anything. I lost my car in the war. I needed it. That was mine. They took it away. I was never compensated. And we got 5,000 schillings for the apartment, for the car, for everything, for clothes, and the Jews got millions, got their businesses, everything, as reparations.

Oh well, I've been through a lot and I've seen a lot, and we had to suffer many hardships. We don't get anything. I served in the German Wehrmacht. What do I get?

All politicians are crooks; there are no greater crooks than politicians. But of course, I vote, and my party, of course, is the Austrian People's Party. It's not really true that my party voted against the monument of Jews scrubbing the streets. I really didn't follow it. They do what they want to do anyway.

I was only six when all that horror happened. It was tough for us, we had nothing to eat, and of course everybody is being blamed now. It was a dark and terrible time for all Austrians because Hitler was a black sheep.

I think that we may have taken these things too lightly for many years. And that's coming back to haunt us. For us that's good. For sure. You have to distinguish now too: Austrians and Germans. There's a basic difference. Let me explain. The Austrian, especially the Viennese, could probably be called a follower. But he doesn't have the consistency that Germans have in everything they do. Let's consider the Jewish affair. In Vienna around 1900, the father of the family cursed the bad Jews at home, and in the evening he met his Jewish friends at the coffeehouse, and they played cards. That's about how we do it.

Is that better or worse than the Germans?

It's completely different. There's another example that I like to tell. The Germans listen to sports. Soccer. There's something at stake, let's say the World Cup. The Germans run, they fight until they die. They give everything. Never an Austrian. At some point he'll think: Is it worth it? Is it not worth it? Then he stops.

That's long done anyway; fifty years already. But a real denazification never happened here, because—there are reasons for that about which I feel uncomfortable talking. From the first moment on there was too much corruption among the antifascists. That's why they depended on the old Nazis who were happy to continue to serve and that was very lucrative. A number of those so-called professional antifascists to whom I never wanted to belong, which is a big mistake because otherwise I would be in a different position today; they really helped.

When Austria thinks back to those terrible times, the Nazi times, has that been overcome?

You can't really come to terms with that, because you are constantly reminded of it.

Sure, that is sad.

We were too young back then to understand all this.

Do you believe that it is dealt with in school enough?

I don't think so.

How about the thing with the Jews? Is that a problem still?

Well, I've never had anything against the Jews and I still don't. When the Reich descended upon us, I can remember how my mother burst into tears.

What do you think? Is the coming to terms with history progressing sufficiently?

No, not at all. Unfortunately, it's been repressed since '45. People believed it was over, the victims of the Third Reich.

Nobody tells the Germans to come to terms. They started the war. What do people tell Czechoslovakia? That's all false propaganda. We are left with the Yugoslavs, the Turks, as foreign workers here in spite of having unemployment. The Nazis came here and then work was promised. What would you say, if you didn't have anything to wear, nothing on at all, and somebody came along and said: "Well, you come to me." Under the worst circumstances you would say: "Well, at least I have shelter."

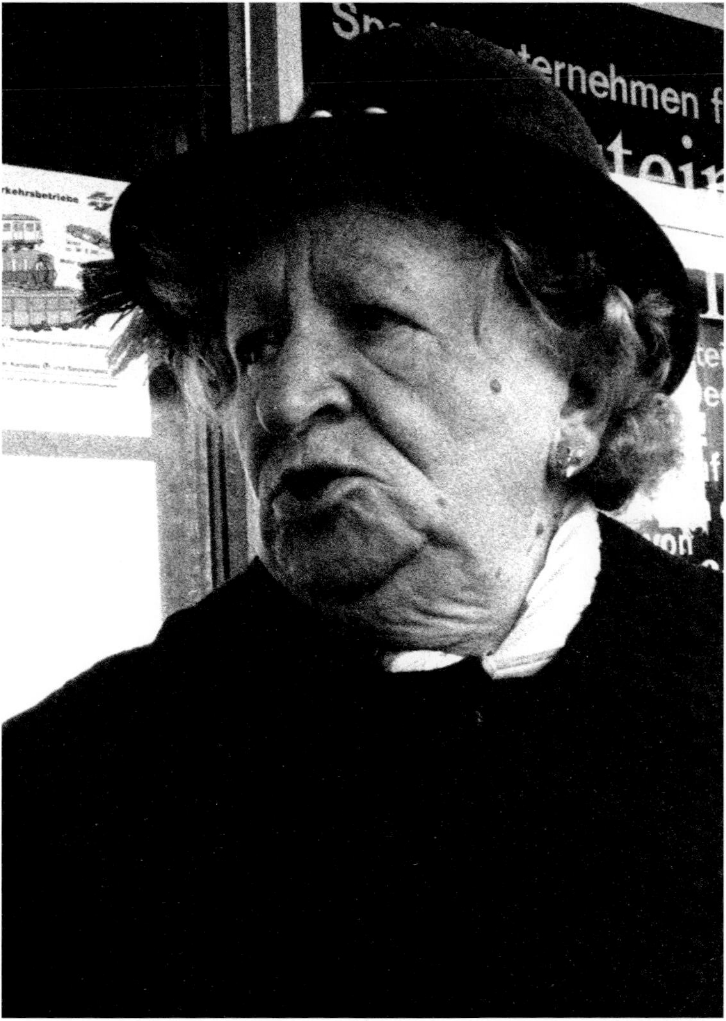
rkehrsbetriebe
ternehmen f

I was born after the Nazi time. I am a cosmopolitan individual, and I can tell you this: Nobody will ever change the problems of Austria. Austrians are 80 percent petty. Just look at me: I have black hair and a black mustache, so you might think I'm an Arab or Jew or God knows what. And I just stood for a very long time in a large hardware store without being waited on. The manager looked at me, then some Austrians—I mean blond people—came in and the manager passed right by me to wait on them. This smallness is not only about Jews or Arabs. It is basic here. It actually makes them act hatefully towards each other. Envy is their number one emotion. I am visiting here and enjoying it, but I am also very glad to go home.

It's said that the foreigners, not the Jews, are the victims now.

Look down to the Afghans, what happens there; that's the same. I believe it happened. I was expelled from Czechoslovakia. I was expelled from my homeland. I can't complain all the time either. We have to pay for what was done to the Jews. I can't say: "Oh God, what happened to me." I am sorry about it.

As far as I know from my interviews with professors, now the venom is against foreigners; then it was against Jews.

That's a very low level of culture. That's people who have no education, who lack the ability to judge because they lack the most primitive preconditions for education.

Believe me, I learned all about what went on. I learned it in school and at the police academy. It disappoints me that people sometimes call me an anti-Semite just because I perform my duty here.

Guard at Jewish Synagogue

You ask how I feel about the 1988 Austrian efforts to get the people in touch with what happened in the Nazi period. Well, the whole thing makes no difference to me. I don't care if people talk about it or not. One should really leave things the way they are. Anyway, it was all before my time.

Austria's largest daily news organ, the *Kronenzeitung*, attacks me in practically every single issue. Last week I was mentioned twice on the first page as "*Geschichtsjüdin*," which means History-Jew, a word that I must say is new to me. They have tried to discredit my research, calling me Jewish, saying "she involved herself so much with Nazi matters that she must be Jewish, and because she is a History-Jew she hated National Socialism. Part two is correct. Part one is not. I am not Jewish.

Erika Weinzierl, distinguished professor of modern history at the University of Vienna and outspoken critic of Nazism in Austria, discusses some difficulties in reaching the public with the truth about Austria's recent history.

The fact alone that so many people died—the suffering, the hunger—that shouldn't happen again, such a thing.

We're really careful not to experience Nazism again. But everything, whether here or there, has its advantages and disadvantages. Back then, the advantage was that we thought we would get more work, and more money, but then came the big disappointment, then the war broke out, etc.

But what about what was done to the Jews here?

Yes, that's bad, very bad that such a thing was done, but it's murder again everywhere, but back then it was very extreme, that should not have happened. I have to be honest, when I heard about it, the war was already over. And I thought that wasn't true, I said, that's impossible. But it was.

But people knew that Jews were taken away.

Oh well, we were told the Jews would get their own country. And I have to admit, when I tell that about myself, we believed it; we are Jews too. My parents, my sons, my brother, and I. And when we weren't Jews they told us that the Nazis were here already. That is to say, Hitler. And when the war was over, we heard about the mass murder.

Maybe it's a good idea that these things are being talked about, but it's such a long, long time ago.

Well, you know, Vienna remains Vienna. Sure, of course, I suppose there's still some anti-Semitism around. You know, *Wien bleibt Wien.*

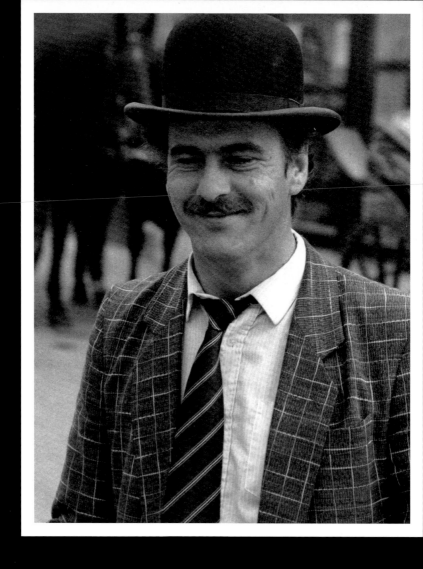

If that came again today, it would be the same again. Look around in the world. Look to Lebanon and such a Khomeini; the poor always pay the price. That's how it was here with the Jews and that's how it always was. Because the rich called it quits. They could have taken the poor with them, they'd have had enough money.

What rich . . .

The Jews who went to America. Why did they leave the poor behind?

The question is: Why were they killed?